THE SINGLE GIRL

B O O K

LIVING THE MOMENT

JENNI STEVENSON

TABLE OF CONTENT

READERS NOTE

You are expected to read through this book with much neutrality and enough positivity within your mind. The book entails a lot and at the same time very easy to understand, above all it was created in a pattern that you can always reflect into the pages at any point in time. Hello single lady, have fun.

CHAPTER ONE

TRIALS OF THE SINGLE GIRL

QUESTIONS YOU NEED TO ASK YOURSELF

The freedom to be single eventually loses all novelty at some point. At some point, you see all your friends joining her social media or going on vacation. I can't seem to attend social events without someone's partner by my side. And you can't help but ask yourself: Why haven't I found anyone yet? Will I stay single forever? Whether you finally find the love of your life doesn't just depend on whether you go on a fixed number of dates each month. You may need to take a step back from dating and ask yourself a few questions to see if your head and heart are really in the right place. Here are the questions:

Did You Leave Your Ex?

We often underestimate how past relationships can affect the way we live and think about the future. And one of the biggest obstacles for most people trying to find a healthy new relationship is the long-term damage they suffered from a previous relationship. Your ex was once someone you gave your all to. I've been in this situation too, and I understand how difficult it can be to move on. That's why I wanted to share what helped me:

A rejuvenating free-breathing video, created by Brazilian shaman Rudá Iandê. Combining breathing with one's knowledge of magic, these exercises aim to restore emotional balance and dissolve anxiety, but above all to reconnect with oneself. Ever since I started the exercises, I feel like I can finally focus on myself instead of my ex. And, I feel like I'm in a better place to create healthy and authentic relationships, especially as the relationship I have with myself is thriving. After all, it's the most important relationship you'll ever have. Do it first, stay true to yourself, and you'll soon attract love back.

Are You Someone Other People Want to Be With?

Being single when you don't want to can be extremely frustrating. You think, "I'm doing everything I can, why is it so hard to find someone to love me?" And you start questioning your self-esteem because maybe you're exposing all your hurts, and even then, no one wants to marry you. But maybe the problem is not your will to love, but your basic personality – the way you act and behave in general. Maybe you can't find someone who wants to love you and accept your love because you're making it hard for people to love you in the first place. So, ask yourself: are you someone other people would love to be around? Are you having trouble making friends? Do you exude positive energy that inspires and enlightens others, or does he turn negative, grumpy, contentious, or unloving? Before anyone can love you, they must love you. But do you love yourself?

Are You Open to New Things?

Humans are creatures of habit. A very extrovert or even a party animal will eventually fall into routines and schedules. The problem with this behavior, however, is that it tends to get too deep into our stubborn everyday lives. Eventually, over time, you'll develop little comfort zones in every aspect of your life, leaving little or no room for new things. Maybe you're just doing what you've been doing for years and you're getting to the point where you can't remember the last time you did something new in your life. So how can you expect to meet the love of your life if you can only walk the paths marked by the footprints of the past? They're not where you've been. If you want to find them, you'll have to go somewhere else and do something else.

Is The Perfect Person Waiting for You?

When you think of the person you want to spend the rest of your life with, what do you think of? What does it look like? How do they act and behave? What is your hobby? what is her temper? How much time have you spent dreaming about this person and trying to embody them in your reality? Having the ideal partner is never a bad thing, but it can sabotage dozens of potential relationships just because they don't fit exactly the way you envisioned. Dream Your Perfect Soulmate Things can create unrealistic expectations for the people around you. You will never give them a chance because they are not the exact match for the man or woman of your dreams. It is time to let go of that ideal partner. You might think it's about settling down with the next person you meet. But it's not. It's about being more open to new possibilities, rather than forcing people to create people who don't exist in the universe.

Do You Know Who You Are and What You Want Out of Your Life?

So many frustrated singles try to date, meet new people, and build relationships that ultimately fail But how much time and energy have you spent on yourself? Some people use relationships as a crutch. Your partner becomes your distraction from yourself and your own life because you don't know who you are or what you want to do with yourself. However, using relationships to fill a void in your life can lead to several toxic and destructive behaviors such as obsession, jealousy, and neediness., can see through all of this. They can see through your attempts to fill the void in your life with a relationship, which pushes them away from you. For this reason, it is important to know yourself before embarking on your journey, including your goals, needs, and personality.

Do You Love Yourself?

No one can love you if you don't love yourself. Do you love the person you see in the mirror? Loving yourself is not easy. No one knows your worst qualities and sins better than you. You've let yourself down too many times, betrayed yourself, and may find it difficult to live with some of the things you've done in the past. If you don't love yourself, you can't get someone to love you. You can use their love to offset feelings of emptiness and even resentment towards yourself, you cannot love others unconditionally and indefinitely. let's move on. Only then can you find people to participate.

Are You Willing to Work for Your Love?

When asked couples who have spent their lives together, "What is the most important thing in a long-lasting relationship?" We will answer something like willingness. We have the idea that love should be easy. And first is that beautiful honeymoon stage. But after the novelty of the relationship wears off, both partners have to deal with the reality that they are spending their lives with completely different people. And no matter how compatible two people are, they will always clash somewhere. This means that there are countless possibilities for you and your partner to argue and possibly break up. If you don't mind. Accommodate your partner, learn to compromise, and make adjustments and changes in small ways to become better companions. your partner.

Are You Actively Working to Become a Healthier and More Attractive Person?

Sure, true love should be more than the surface, but people who don't care about themselves No one wants to spend their life with Just like you want an attractive, fit, and healthy partner, so do others. When was the last time you went to the gym? Have you ever counted your calories? Can you cook and do you think about the nutrition of food when you eat it? Are you the type of person who cares about your health and well-being? You don't have to be an Instagram model to find a relationship...but you should do everything you can to look clean and cent. Taking care of your body not only makes it easier to attract potential partners but italsonspires them to be their best selves.

Do You Push People Away When They Get Too Close?

It's easy to say you're not compatible with anyone without realizing that you might neglect the effort it takes to get close to someone. Vulnerability is hard. It's hard to open up to someone. This is especially true in the modern dating scene where everyone seems willing to go for the next best thing. Learning how to balance intimacy with absolute vulnerability is an essential skill. Revealing cards too easily risk scaring them away. At the same time, if you draw too much affection from her, she may think you're not interested. It's time for her to open up and let people into your life. Shared humor and similar tastes can only go so far. If you want to connect with other humans and find potential partners, we will do the necessary work to make it happen. We tend to have the notion that romantic connections are fleeting and anything less than that isn't worth pursuing. need a job.

Do You Avoid Challenges Because You Cannot Accept Rejection?

I am afraid to appear outside. The thought of opening up and being rejected by someone sounds dreadful, but it's part of the process. Some are lucky, but for most of us, it takes more than a few bad dates to find the love of our lives. Bad dates are an inevitable part of this journey.

It makes the destination more worthwhile. Maybe you have a habit of dismissing others easily or being mindful of what they have to offer. Unconsciously, these are your coping mechanisms. There is no need to deal with the possibility of refusal, as there may be. Your relationship will never work if you don't take risks. The right person for you may be closer than you think, but you risk missing out on opportunities because you're too scared to participate in the process. Rejection is a normal part of dating. Please don't take it personally. Don't be discouraged.

Are There Other Areas in Your Life That You Would Like to Prioritize First?

Too many people use relationships as a crutch. They think society is a band-aided solution to their problems, which affects their chances of dating that special someone. The reason why you are not having luck in relationships may be because you are not ready for a relationship. Loving yourself is not the only factor in establishing a healthy relationship with yourself. You may be dealing with past baggage from a previous relationship that is preventing you from being your best self in new relationships. Become more aware of your place in psychological and emotional development. You may be unconsciously projecting personal problems onto others, limiting your ability to connect and communicate with those around you. Things like job security and financial stability are also important factors when dating someone. People who want to settle down often look to people who have more or less a life together. People want to date people who have something to offer. Do you have interesting hobbies? Do you have passions that you can share with someone? Focusing on self-development will propel you forward and make you a more attractive person.

Have You Forgotten How to Flirt?

Flirting is a clear way to show interest. Directness is important in the game of attraction. How else will someone know that you're interested in them romantically? Playful banter sets the tone for getting to know someone and building a relationship with them. It's a way to show off who you are and prove that you're not boring. As important as it is to be open, flirting is also a key part of being attractive.

Some friendships don't go further than that because one or both of the people involved don't feel sexual chemistry. Too many people end up in the friend zone because they don't take the relationship to the next level. If good dates end with "I would love to be friends," you probably need to work on your flirting skills.

Do You Easily Fall to Bed?

You might think that having a lot of different sexual partners would help you find true love faster. After all, the more people you sleep with, the more you can find out if you are compatible with them. In reality, this could make it harder for you to find someone you could be with for a long time.

The way people date today makes it easy to get what you want out of a relationship without always putting in the work. You could meet someone on the same day, talk, and sleep with them, but you might never see them again. If you make it too easy for someone to sleep with you, they won't have any reason to stick around or try harder. When you set the bar too low, they know they can get the benefits without committing to you.

Do people often stop talking to you after your second or third date? How often do you fall in love with someone, only for them to break up with you a few weeks later? If you've been dating pretty much a new guy every week, you might want to think about how casual you are with sex.

When you share intimacy with someone you care about, it feels so much better.

If Someone Has One Flaw, Do You Give Up on Them?

App-based dating makes it seem like there are endless ways to meet people. Not happy with where the talk is going? Separate them and try again. Did they do something a bit strange?

Ghost them and don't talk to them ever again. One of the biggest problems with dating in the modern world is that it makes people take each other for granted. People are less likely to stay with someone and work through their flaws, no matter how small, because they have lost hope and are sure that The One is just a swipe away.

In real life, there is no perfect relationship. Even if two people are perfect for each other, they will still have some awkward moments in the beginning. Even if you don't like something about a person, that doesn't mean that you can't find a way to get along. Too many people find the smallest things wrong and use that as a reason to break up.

This leads to a cycle of swiping and hoping that the next person you talk to is perfect.

Are You Ready to Commit to Someone?

To be successful in a relationship, you must desire to be in one. Unknowingly, you may be conveying a lack of commitment, which would account for the failure of your relationship attempts. It's okay if you don't want a relationship. Do not be persuaded by your peers into believing that everyone requires this type of arrangement.

Perhaps this is the time in your life when you want to "shop around." Perhaps you want to use this time to meet new people without necessarily settling down because you're still recovering from prior hurts. It's crucial to know what your true desires are. This enables you to establish goals for yourself. By doing this, you can stop yourself from feeling frustrated when you realize that you're not developing in the conventional sense.

You may better navigate other people's emotions and establish connections with like-minded individuals by being aware of where you stand in terms of relationships.

Do You Think You're Getting Better Every Day?

Are you being the best you can be for others? Do you take care of your body well enough for others to find you physically appealing? Do you have interests, a future goal for your work, and just some basic topics to discuss and offer the other person?

Value proposals are the foundation of dating. Finding the ideal partner is unlikely if you're a 28-year-old loser who lives in your parents' basement and spends much of your free time playing video games. You must be the person who will attract the individuals you want to be with if you want to attract them.

This entails making an effort to advance oneself. If you're not having much luck finding dates, use this as a clue that you need to start improving. Get into a new pastime, work on your body, and enhance your social skills.

Do You Comprehend Their Needs?

You need to understand what guys want from a relationship with you if you're a woman wondering why you don't have a boyfriend. And more than previously believed, males are more influenced by biological inclinations in their romantic relationships, according to new research. Men in particular want to take care of and safeguard you. Their biology is strongly ingrained with this drive. Men have desired to defend the women in their lives ever since humans first began to evolve.

Men still desire to do this in modern times. Of course, you may not require him as well, but that does not imply that guys do not care about you. Their DNA is programmed to accomplish this. Making your husband feel important will trigger his protective instincts and the most virtuous side of his masculinity. It will most critically let loose his intense sensations of attraction.

the real kicker? If this thirst is not quenched, a man won't fall for a lady. This scientific justification of what guys desire intrigues me as a unique perspective on what motivates men romantically. James Bauer, a relationship psychologist, was the one who first introduced me to this innate inclination. It is no secret that instincts govern human behavior, but James was the first to apply this to male and female romantic relationships.

Do You Give People A Chance?

Because they never give others an opportunity, some people are still single. They refuse dates and don't spend the time getting to know someone. Is he fond of me? This is a question that every woman has posed to a man at least once. To determine whether he likes you, I've created a fun quiz.

Try a different tactic, be honest, and give other people a chance if you're like this. The future? Some wonderful love tales start in an unexpected way. If you allow others into your heart, someone may eventually decide to move in and remain.

Are You Overly Reliant?

Stop relying on others all the time and clinging to them like glitter. Neediness is not appealing. Be self-reliant and demonstrate to people that you are in charge of your own life. Cut that. You don't have to assert your authority in front of others. simply lead your own life. Spend some time by yourself and learn to manage your affairs alone.

It's not necessary to chase after the right individual.

Do You Interact with New People?

Look, it might be difficult to find the time to meet new people, especially if your schedule is constantly full. However, fully cutting oneself off from social interaction could have a bad impact on both your social life and your prospects of finding your future spouse. Spending time with others can help you strike a healthy balance between job and social life.

Be available to socialize and sibe ngle. If you don't occasionally leave the house, how on earth would you meet new people? You miss out on unexpected meetings, introductions, and more even if you use online dating to discover date partners.

Are You Enjoying Being Single?

It takes time to discover the proper person to be with, so don't panic if you've tried the last 10 advice suggestions but are still single. It's best to improve yourself and relish being single in the interim. Spend time with your loved ones, socialize with your friends, and engage in activities that bring you joy. Even though traveling, you can discover how vast the earth is. You'll meet someone soon, and being single won't be a problem any longer. Recognize that someone is out there who is intended for you and that meeting them is only a question of time.

Do You Inevitably Fall in Love?

If you fall head over heels in love with everyone you meet, it could be difficult for you to find someone to be in a relationship with. This screams desperation, and no one loves a desperate person. Always keep in mind that true love and fulfillment require time. When it comes to creating a solid relationship, the concept of "love at first sight" is untrue.

Now what? No one has to remain single indefinitely. These 23-pointers should inspire you to put yourself out there and discover the appropriate partner. But I believe many women miss out on one essential component of successful relationships: understanding how guys think. It can seem tough to get a guy to open up and tell you how he acts. And because of this, developing a meaningful connection can be quite challenging.

Men perceive the world differently than you do, let's face it. And because of this, it may be challenging to have a deeply passionate romantic relationship—something that all men secretly desire. In my experience, sex, conversation, or going on romantic dates are never the missing pieces in a relationship. All of these factors are significant, but they don't always determine whether a relationship will succeed. Understanding what motivates guys is essentially the missing piece.

The new film from relationship psychologist James Bauer will enable you to comprehend men's romantic tendencies and the kinds of women they are attracted to. James discloses a "hidden element" in relationships that few women are aware of but which is the secret of a man's love and commitment.

CHAPTER TWO

REASONS FOR BEING SINGLE

KARMIC REASONS FOR BEING SINGLE YOU NEED TO KNOW ABOUT

Do you believe that the reason you're single is that you haven't found the proper person? There are additional factors to take into account.

Here are 10 karmic factors that you should be aware of.

You Don't Think You're Deserving

Many single people may assert that this is untrue and that they do feel deserving of love. If this is you, may I ask if you think you are deserving? Examine your life and be sincere in your response regarding your self-care.

Do you:

every night, get adequate rest.

Eat a healthy, balanced diet.

Regular exercise

Keep a thought journal.

Take some time to unwind and relax.

compassion toward oneself

If you selected "yes" to the majority or all of these questions, you are demonstrating to the universe that you think you are deserving by looking after yourself. On the other side, you give the message that these things don't belong to you if you don't take care of yourself. If that's the case, you can be sure that a respectable companion won't help you find love. Indeed, loving oneself comes first.

Do you ever wonder why you don't feel deserving? You may suffer from ingrained problems including low self-esteem and behavioral problems, according to a PsychTest.com survey. We should all believe that we are deserving of love, therefore get the assistance you require from a qualified specialist to put you on the right track.

Being Single Cannot Make You Happy

I'll share a tale about an older colleague. She held that love was necessary for self-fulfillment. She was misled by a widespread notion that we have seen in romantic comedies and advertisements. Know you who it is? Many of us, according to Rudá, chase love indestructivelyecause because we aren't taught how to love ourselves first. She claims that our capitalist society's hunger for love led her to spend years believing it to be a delusion. Love is a marketing gimmick for goods.

She is one of many people who fell for the princess and the prince plot, which is based on the notion that someone must complete you. She has been in romances every year since she was 17 years old. Over the past four decades, she has only ever been by herself for approximately a year at a time. Yes, forty years. She didn't believe she could live a happy single life, so the universe has now made sure she does. A year ago, she ended her third long-term relationship because she was fed up with her narcissistic husband's emotional abuse.

She couldn't have gotten a worse partner from the universe, so she's going to stay single for a while. She's had enough bad boyfriends to last a lifetime. Trust me, she's been through enough. Now, she thinks that you have to be a whole person before you can look for love. She tells me that she now knows that everything she was looking for was inside of her all along. Also, she tells me that if she meets someone again in the future, it will be a meeting of two whole people and nothing else.

No more codependency.

How will this affect you?

Perhaps the Universe wants you to be single so that you can grow as a person. There's a chance that it's pushing you through the uncomfortable to help you move up in your life and put that energy back into you.

You Need to Be by Yourself to Get Better

You may be single right now because you need to heal or because you need to stop believing the myth that you need a partner to be whole. This doesn't have to have anything to do with a previous relationship. It could be something that happened to you when you were young and that you have been carrying around with you for years or even decades.

Working through these will require you to think about yourself and maybe even get help from a professional, but it will be worth it because it will give you more space. You see, this space could make it possible for you to meet the person you've been looking for. I've always found that relationships have shown up when I was ready for them.

I have to be honest: after my long-term relationship ended, I moved into a new one very quickly. But the truth is that I was sad about the end of the relationship while I was still in it. I knew where it was going, so I started to move on in my mind. In my own life, I've learned to trust the Universe's timing, and I had not to doubt that my new relationship came about at the right time, even though it seemed a little early to other people.

Don't worry about when things will happen. If your partner isn't here right now, you should look inside.

You Don't Believe in The Concept of Love

When someone talks about love, do you roll your eyes? This could be why you haven't been with anyone for so long. You're making it hard for yourself to find love because you don't believe it's possible. Ask yourself if you think it's impossible to find a great person and fall in love with them.

See what you think about that question. When love doesn't believe in you, it's easy to get angry and feel like you can't do anything. You might even want to give up on love and throw in the towel. I want to suggest that you try something else. I learned this from Rudá Iandê, a world-famous shaman. He showed me that the way to find love and closeness is not what our culture has taught us.

Many of us hurt ourselves and play tricks on ourselves for years, making it harder to find a partner who can truly make us happy. The things Rudá taught me made me see things in a whole new way. While I was watching, I felt like for the first time, someone understood how hard it was for me to find and keep love, and for the first time, someone gave me a real, practical way to get over the idea that true love was impossible to find.

Your Goal Right Now Is to Serve the World

When I think about this point, I think of a good friend of mine who works as a spiritual coach. She helps women work through their pain and find inner peace so they don't have to carry the weight of their traumas with them all the time. She helps other people every day of her life. I know that she puts a lot into her work and that it gives her a lot of pleasure.

She tells me that she is doing what she was meant to do. My friend has only had one long-term relationship since she started working in this field. That lasted a year, but it ended because he hurt her bywithhat what he did. I've noticed that she has very strong limits and doesn't let any crap in. If she clocks on to someone bad, they are out. I like this because she has taught me how to be.

Now: I'm telling you this story because I can see that her work, her mission, is a very important thing to her. She doesn't put dating at the top of her list of things to do. I've seen her go out on casual dates with people she's met in real life, but she doesn't use apps to look for Mr. Right. She is busy living out her purpose and using her gift to help people around the world. Does this sound right to you? It could be a big reason why you don't have a partner yet.

The world needs your gifts, and it doesn't want you to waste your energy on someone else who probably isn't worth it.

A Toxic Relationship Is Difficult to Leave Behind

It's likely accurate if you believe you were in a toxic relationship. You can have a lower likelihood of finding someone else because of the toxic hangover. Even though they may have long since left your life, their lingering bad vibes can still be keeping you single. I am aware that it might be difficult to let go of someone; I have been there.

Even though we are aware that toxic people are not beneficial to Fotos, this is nonetheless applicable to them. First of all, be kind to yourself for choosing to stay in that partnership. then decide it's time to spiritually sever your relationship with that person. ViA visualizations are a potent tool that can assist you in letting go of someone and moving on.

You may begin by performing a "cord-cutting" meditation, in which you picture cutting the rope that binds you to your ex-flame with scissors or even imagining using a blowtorch to separate you two. You can also utilize symbolic letter writing as a potent method to let go of a previous connection.

Write out everything you want to tell your ex-partner, s if they are going to read it. Instead of sending it to them, burn this letter as part of your ritual of letting go. Allow this gesture to assist you in letting go of them by wishing them well and sending them love and light.

Your ideal companion might then show up as a result of this.

You Choose the Wrong Karmic Partner

I feel like I'm now involved in a karmic relationship. I can assure you that it is equally turbulent and intense as you may have heard. See, I genuinely believe my current relationship is in my life to advance my growth. We've been learning a lot from one another and have both advanced in many different ways. It's been challenging and contentious, but it's also been a remarkably cathartic and therapeutic relationship. I wouldn't have it any other way since it allows for growth. According to Anna Schreuder's article for Nomads, karmic mates aren't all that beneficial for us if you haven't met the proper one.

Right now, my partner and I are figuring out how to deal with the triggers that we constantly discovering in one another. I can tell you that there is a lot of introspection and thoughtful discussion. We both intend to improve our connection and take advantage of any forthcoming teachings. This has required me to examine the baggage I've been carrying, such as my fears and trust concerns. Although unpleasant, it was crucial for my development.

Now, if you keep attracting partners that are causing the same problems for you, it's time to consider the karmic lesson in this. According to Schreuderr, noticing similar patterns in many relationships could be an indication that you need to stop a karmic cycle.

One approach to accomplish this is to think while you are alone.

You Simply Aren't Prepared for A Relationship Just Yet

Speaking about the fort: Being in a relationship is difficult work, despite the cliché. In my own experience, I find relationships to be tremendously fulfilling, but I'd be lying if I said they weren't difficult and labor-intensive. You may be single because the Universe recognizes that you are not yet prepared to commit to someone who requires this kind of time and effort.

Consider this a time to reflect on the self-improvement work you need to do. Before you can be in a position where you are prepared for a relationship, what aspects of your life do you need to work on? Can self-love be the cause? How does this affect you? The chances are that your karmic reasons for remaining single in the first place will likely vanish once you reach a state of contented singledom.

You're Still Grieving the Loss of Your Past Relationship

How long does it take to get over someone? I found myself asking after splitting up with my ex. I thought my suffering would never be over. I was in such continual discomfort and was beside myself. Looking back on it, it still seems strange. At times, I had the sensation that my heart was about to burst. It was too soon to expect the grief to be passed when I was looking for this, just a few months after my split.

According to one research study, it can take between three and six months to move past an ex-spouse, and if you two were married, it could even take up to 18 months. If you fall within these timeframes, you may be still mourning the end of your relationship.

Grieving happens in stages. It contains:

Denial

Anger Bargaining

Depression

Acceptance

Allow yourself to go through the motions; just because someone is still alive doesn't mean that you can't express symbolic grief for their absence from your life. You can meet someone fresh when you're ready by accepting yourself and going on with your life.

You Haven't Forgiven Yourself for Something

It's hard to believe that you're the reason you're still single, especially if you're going on dates and trying to meet someone. Maybe the last time you were in a relationship, it ended because of something you did. This is what happened with my current boyfriend and one of his previous partners. Even though they had only been together for three months, she wanted him to make a promise. Because he was afraid, he wasn't ready to give her what she wanted, so she left his life and didn't look back.

After that, he spent a year beating himself up over what had happened, and he went on dates to keep himself busy. They got nowhere. He was trying to find a partner, but nothing was working out. He started talking to a therapist, who helped him figure out how to forgive himself and put the situation to rest. This meant that I had to write her a letter. Even though a symbolic letter is just as strong, he sent it to her. Even though she didn't answer, this action helped him get some closure and understand why he couldn't commit at the time.

One year later, when I met him, he was ready to make a commitment to someone. He had finally forgiven himself and let go of the pain he had been carrying.

How will this affect you? Trust the way life works! Even if the order of events doesn't make sense at the time, everything will make sense as time goes on.

CHAPTER THREE

HOW TO MAKE PEACE WITH BEING SINGLE

KEY STEPS TO MAKING PEACE WITH BEING SINGLE

It can be hard to be single. This is especially true if you don't have a romantic partner but wish you did. If people keep telling you to "chill out" and be patient while you're going through this, you might be sick of hearing that. How to accept being single: 11 important steps

Don't Be Perfect

I think that romantic love is real. I also think that we only meet a small number of people with whom we can have long-term relationships. Still, believing in a soulmate, twin flame, or perfect partner can cause a lot of pain. Justin Brown, a co-founder of Idea pod, talks about how we often have so many hopes for finding "the one" that we end up being very disappointed when things don't go as planned. We're divided, alone, and lost. One of the best ways to deal with being single is to break this rule.

Realize that even if some of your ideals are true, the grass is always greener on the other side. As Justin says in this article, it's great to want a partner, and it's a healthy tension to feel torn between being happy being single and wanting a partner.

If you're sad about being single, you need to accept and deal with that sadness. If you want to be okay with being single, you need to accept how you feel about it on the inside. Even though it may sound strange, some people find being in relationships very uncomfortable, even when they are in love. Even though they feel stifled, they often have to make peace to stay in a relationship.

Everyone goes on their path.

Look Into Troubled Relationships

Seeing other people in bad relationships has never made me happier or more at peace with being single. Have you ever seen a couple of fight in public or give each other dirty looks while out shopping? From miles away, you can feel the anger and stress. Look at Johnny Depp and Amber Heard, whose abusive relationship was aired for the whole world to see. Even the richest and most famous people feel pain and confusion when a relationship goes bad. If you're single and feeling like you're missing out, look at the people who aren't single but wish they were. They would switch places with you right away. There are also plenty of happy relationships that seem to be pretty good, but the point is that it's not a sure thing.

Also, many people start out happy but quickly fall off a terrible cliff. This isn't meant to make you happy about being single for the rest of your life, and it might not fix deeper feelings of loneliness and rejection, but it can help you see some of the good things about your situation.

Discover How to Find True Love and Intimacy

Finding love and intimacy is challenging, but many of us make it considerably harder than necessary by lying to ourselves. Have you ever wondered why love is so difficult? Why can't it turn out the way you pictured growing up? Or at least be logical... It's simple to get upset and even feel helpless when you've been alone for a long time and are uncomfortable with it. You might even feel the need to give up on love and throw in the towel. Contrary to what we have been culturally conditioned to think, there is another way to find love and intimacy. For years, many of us deceive ourselves and self-destruct, preventing us from finding a mate who can fulfill us. We end up being stuck in bad relationships or meaningless meetings, never really finding what we're seeking, and feeling miserable about things like protracted dry spells in love or being compelled to accept the first person who approaches us and expresses interest.

Rather than the real person, we fall in love with an idealized version of them. We attempt to "repair" our spouses but end up severing bonds.

We search for someone to "complete" us, only to crumble in their presence and feel twice as horrible. If you're tired of disappointing dates, fruitless hookups, trying relationships, and repeatedly having your dreams dashed, you need to alter your perception of yourself. You won't be let down, I promise.

Be Receptive to Possibilities

It's crucial to be a little impulsive in life and see what transpires. In daily life, you never know who you'll run across or what can transpire. As Justin points out, our natural and enjoyable experience of life may be hampered if we overcommit to a goal of remaining single or being in a relationship. Making peace with how much of life is beyond our control is essential to coming to terms with being single as well. You might find the love of your life just when you thought there was no hope left. They could betray you in a way that takes years to recover from just when you believe you've found a companion who genuinely understands you. Keep an open mind and avoid counting your chickens before they are even born.

You might be single right now and have been for some time. You never know when it will be your turn, yet the magic happens every day. Love, as they say, often shows up when you least expect it. This leads me to my next point.

Uninstall Dating Apps Like Tinder

Nowadays, dating applications like Tinder are the only way to meet new people. If you're looking for romance, why in the world would you remove them? You might at the very least wind up having a good time with a handsome stranger, don't you think? Everyone has the right to use whatever applications they want and to live their own lives. I think they often lead to encounters with a lot of people we wouldn't seek out or be drawn to in our daily lives, making them addictive and unsatisfying.

Apps frequently connect people who, for various reasons, don't want to be single. That desire to be in a relationship or at the very least be open to one should be acceptable and lovely. It's okay to want a relationship or a date. The issue is that sense of inner inadequacy that frequently accumulates along with looking for a new spouse. Instead of meeting a new person you'd be pleased to name your girlfriend or boyfriend, you encounter someone who is incredibly insecure about being single and makes you question their value or consider how they might be manipulating you.

That has been my experience, at least. According to a woman who used dating apps, "I thought I was in control of my dating life when I used dating apps, but I discovered that I had ceded control to the algorithmic whims of apps driven by big data, and propelled by my own excessive and increasing desperation, I descended into mindless swiping that left me more dissatisfied than when I started."

Concentrate On Work and Projects

Focusing on work and projects you're enthusiastic about is another suggestion I have for adjusting to being single. Even better, you can frequently meet that particular someone by pursuing your passions and concentrating on your life goals. Consider getting a second, more social part-time work if your current position keeps you caged up a lot. Get out and meet individuals with similar interests!

You may remain single, but as a bachelor or bachelorette, you are likely to enjoy a far larger social network and more fulfilling existence. Even better, you will build bridges for your social life and personal growth in a variety of novel ways. This can involve starting your own business, pursuing higher education, or any number of other ideas that can help you connect with others and achieve your objectives.

Create Your Narrative

Too frequently, we subconsciously live our lives in accordance with the values and objectives of others. In my situation, I always believed that I would meet "the one" and live happily ever after from an early age. This belief was not conditioned or taught to me; rather, it was something that my imaginative and idealistic youthful self-developed. I was told by authority people, parents, and relatives that marriage and relationships are extremely difficult and shouldn't be the goal of life, thus my upbringing is somewhat averse to individuals who are trained to place a high value on pair bonding.

Regardless of how you were raised or what principles you were taught, make sure you're not living another person's tale and calling it your own. This is especially prevalent when we reenact the stories of our parents, seeking or rejecting love to deal with the unresolved trauma they left us with as a result of their marital problems.

Two Halves or Two Wholes?

The concept of discovering our "other half" dates back to ancient Greece and to the Garden of Eden in the Bible. It is a romantic and fateful idea, but it can also be subtle disempowerment. How can you be successful in life if you're just half a person till you meet your other half?

It is romantic in a sense, but tragic as well. Consider yourself as a whole individual who is striving to become even more well-rounded and self-reliant. This is a more effective approach to making peace with being single. There's always room for a partner in crime, but you don't need one. This is the correct mindset for accepting singlehood. To view yourself as having more than you need and to be open to the possibility of accepting someone who has their own life and is not codependent.

As for physical desires and needs? This energy can frequently be channeled into your work-related passions and endeavors. Emotional needs and a sense of isolation? This is when we are formed into the person we'll become, and these hard times often look worthwhile in retrospect.

Get Some Help Outside

Being single isn't the end of the world. It might be a fun and stimulating moment. Many people come to the realization that being single for so long actually prepared them for finding a compatible partner. All that time spent growing deeper and experiencing ups and downs helped them become the ideal match for their future partner. Nevertheless, there may not always appear to be any hope for the future. The hunt for love and relationships can be difficult and complex. There are moments when you reach a wall and are genuinely unsure of what to do next. I admit that before I really used it, I had my doubts about seeking assistance from outside sources.

The finest website I've found for love counselors who don't just talk is Relationship Hero. They have experienced it all and are knowledgeable on how to handle challenging circumstances, such as accepting being single and making it a strength rather than a weakness. Since there were so many couples around and I was single at the time, I tried them last year. I wanted to talk to a professional about my feelings and what they signified because I felt like the only person who wasn't involved in a beautiful romance. My coach was considerate, took the time to comprehend my particular circumstances, and offered genuinely beneficial guidance.

You can speak with a licensed relationship coach in just a few minutes to receive guidance that is specifically tailored to your needs.

Socialize With Other Singles

I used to participate in a program called YSA (Young Single Adults). The idea is straightforward: unmarried young people meet up, study the Bible and the Book of Mormon, and form friendships. In order to connect and socialize with other single people, try to look for possibilities regardless of your culture or religious background. These could be meetups for hikes, solitary retreats, or many more places that cater more to lone travelers. You'll realize there are many excellent single people out there and you're not alone once you're around more single people.

Find Your Uncomfortable Zone.

Our greatest significant growth often takes place in our comfort zone. It happens when we turn away from ease and pleasure and run toward difficulty and harsh reality. Finding inspiration in the dissatisfaction you have when being single can help you become a more genuine and motivated person is what it means to make peace with being single. Focus on that nagging feeling that you're missing out on life rather than "thinking positively" or picturing your ideal future partner. That nagging notion that you'll "always" be alone... Then use that energy to complete a killer exercise, create a novel piece of software, assist an elderly guy in crossing the street, or even provide a friend relationship advice. Face the problem of being single head-on rather than avoiding it.

Don't concentrate on it, but also don't avoid it. What is, is what is.

Avoid Pushing It!

Ironically, accepting and acknowledging your uncomfortable sentiments about being single is a key component of coming to terms with it. Nobody has the right to pressure you into having a certain emotion or not. A valid feeling is being bothered by being unmarried. You don't have to accept something you don't want to, as one relationship expert put it.

Maybe one day, but for now, everything feels just good! To want someone in your life is NOT a sign of weakness. Making peace with being single requires first letting go of your annoyance with it. That's fine, and as you concentrate on following some of the advice I've provided above, the notion that you're losing out on something by being single will probably start to fade.

CHAPTER FOUR

GETTING OVER SOMEONE YOU NEVER DATED

WAYS TO GET OVER SOMEONE YOU NEVER DATED (COMPREHENSIVE LIST)

It may seem bizarre to be obsessed with a relationship you've never experienced. But feelings, especially love, are not rational. But if you don't take action to move past that individual, you'll be stuck for the rest of your life. In a sense, you need to close this door before another one can open. Ideally, the "new door" will lead to a romantic relationship! Thank goodness, help does go a long way. And in this chapter, we'll cover how to move on from someone you've never dated.

THE CAUSES OF YOUR IMPASSE

Prior to offering advice on how to move on from someone you've never dated, it's critical to recognize these factors because they are essential to your future success. However, it should be noted that this list of causes is by no means complete. Instead, use it as a springboard for considering your justifications.

They Are Now the Center of Attention

You have probably put this person on a pedestal, which is one very good reason why you just couldn't move on from them. You've observed and are enamored with their positive qualities while downplaying or disregarding their negative ones. This frequently occurs in regular relationships as well as in crushes on celebrities. Additionally, you become focused on the idea of "getting" someone after you transform a reachable individual into a flawless superstar. This is typical and the most probable cause. When you've never been together, how can you possibly recognize the negative aspects?

People Have Said You Two Would Get Along Well

Another reason you might find it difficult to let go of someone is peer pressure. Even while at first you might have laughed it off, you eventually come to believe that maybe they are right and you would be fantastic together. But after that, it becomes difficult to contact that person. Perhaps they have other priorities or are in love with someone else. You're left with "what-ifs," wondering if your loved ones didn't see something special developing.

You Seek to Fill a Vacuum in Your Heart Because You Are Lonely

Maybe you've recently recovered from a disastrous split. Perhaps you've been forced to watch your friends get married and have children while you've been there without even one date. There is a gaping, painful hole in your heart that cries out to be filled, whether it is caused by one of the aforementioned factors or something else. As a result, you cling to the first person to express affection for you or who you perceive to be close by. They eventually take over your thinking and develop into a unique individual. They easily lose their value and cannot be replaced.

However, despite the fact that you could believe your obsession is with them, the reality is that it is with you and your desire for approval.

You've Actually Given It Your All

There's a chance that perhaps, just perhaps, you overreacted or jumped to conclusions. Perhaps when you tried to ask them out, they seemed reluctant, and you mistakenly assumed that meant they said no. Or perhaps you didn't even ask them out; you just believed they were already engaged when you spotted them walking with someone else.

What if they are only uneasy and still like you? Although it may be frightening, it is wise to reconsider your perception of the situation and give it a try before giving it up. If anything, failing to consider all of your options will leave you with regrets and long-lasting "what-ifs." Naturally, that entails doing every effort to ensure your success. Additionally, relationship coaches with extensive experience can teach you a lot. While the major strategies for getting over someone you've never dated are covered in this article, it can be beneficial to discuss your situation with a relationship coach.

You Gave Them a Lot of Attention and Effort

The sunk-cost fallacy asserts that individuals who have put a lot of time and effort into something won't let go of it even when it is obvious that it won't work out. This holds for a variety of aspects of life, including work, the arts, and, yes, relationships. Perhaps you had worried endlessly about them. Maybe you gave them a lot of gifts and supported them during some difficult moments. Maybe you were on the verge of dating too.

You've spent most of your time with them—in your brain. However, they either opted to date someone else or had to leave, leaving you to struggle with the realization that your efforts were in vain.

You Have Low Self-Esteem

You may become emotionally attached to someone and become obsessed with them if you lack self-esteem, which is a major contributing factor. You're inclined to cling to the first person who exhibits the slightest sign of affection—even if it's merely friendly—when you don't have much self-confidence. Even if they aren't long-term health benefits for you, it doesn't matter. All that counts to that needy part of you is that they made you feel validated. And ultimately, you'll be so preoccupied with them that you might easily persuade yourself that there isn't anyone else like them—that no one else will ever give you their attention.

HOW TO MOVE ON FROM A PERSON YOU'VE NEVER DATED

I thus hope you took a moment to consider the causes of your extreme stuckness. The fantastic first step, it's now time for you to take action.

Remove Them from Your Life.

You need to create some distance between yourself and them so that you aren't constantly reminded of them. Cut them out of your life immediately if they aren't that interested in talking to you or engaging with you. And one of the first steps you may do to do that is to erase their number, followed by social media unfriending, unfollowing, and blocking. You don't want them to interact with your posts or appear on your timeline. You won't be able to remove them from your mind in that manner.

Now, this is obviously not simple. It's similar to giving up any addiction. Set a date to stop them completely so that you may be kinder to yourself. Spend as much time as you want to obsess over them in the days leading up to that. then 100% stop.

If You Can't Leave Them, Keep Your Distance

Sometimes, you can't just stop talking to them. Maybe your are good friends and you just want to get rid of your feelings for them without losing their friendship. If you want to get over your feelings, it could be because they are getting in the way of your friendship. Here, you can't just vanish into thin air or block them out of the blue. You should instead go talk to them. Tell them how you feel and that you can't be around them until you can handle your feelings. After that, you can delete their number and turn off their social media accounts until you're ready to meet up again.

Remind Yourself That They're Still Human

If part of the issue is that you have idealized them and put them on a pedestal, an answer is to remind yourself that they're human, too. After all, nobody is without flaws. They won't be the perfect person you imagine them to be, and being with them won't be as wonderful as you think it will be. They have flaws, and those flaws will hit you right in the face when you have to deal with them. This makes things worse. For the same reason, people say, "Never meet your heroes."

Think about the times they actually did something wrong, like forgetting their car keys or buying a whole truckload of rice by accident. Even though this might seem cute at first, if you have to deal with it for a few years, it will get old. And if your brain is still too blinded by love to see their flaws, just imagine them doing bad things like being rude to their parents or not wiping their poop well. I know it might seem silly, but it's a psychological trick that works for some people.

Work To Keep Yourself Busy

When your mind isn't busy, it's easy to get lost in obsessive thoughts. You'll think about them over and over again because you have the time to do so. So, you should find something to do. And besides your job, what else is a better way to spend your time and energy? Focus on your work and don't let anything else get in the way, and you'll do well. You might even call it a little bit of spice. Think about it: if you're successful and the best at what you do, people are missing out. You go from being the person who was turned down for a date to the person who turns people down.

Spend Time on Your Hobbies

Another good idea is to spend time on your hobbies. Like throwing yourself into work, you get to keep your mind busy. But hobbies are also about something else. They are what you like to do and what makes you happy. Your hobbies help you turn your interests into something that makes you feel good about yourself. They also make you a more interesting person. You just have more to talk about than people who don't do anything outside of work. Go back to drawing, reading, playing guitar, or even doing crossword puzzles. When you start to think about the person you like, go straight to your hobbies.

Get Rid of Your Mementos

You probably have a few things that remind you of them, like a weighted blanket they gave you or a book they told you to read. You might also have pictures of you two together. Throw these cute things away. Put these reminders somewhere you won't see or think about them for a while. Things like pictures are easy to throw away. Just get rid of them. It's harder to move things like books, blankets, and cups. It wouldn't make much sense to throw them away, but you can give them to a friend to keep until they're no longer important to you.

Open Yourself Up to New People

The best approach to moving on from someone is to just find new people to be interested in. Be open to meeting new people. Even while it may sound unromantic to think of love in that way, emotions can be erratic like that. Fortunately, letting go of someone you've never had is simpler than letting go of someone you did date for a while. Look through profiles and make an effort to get to know people. You could be startled to learn that there are other interesting people in the world besides your object of passion. Enough folks are seeking for that if all you want is a brief scrap in the hay. The same goes for people seeking committed relationships. It will at the very least serve as a reminder that there are other fish in the sea even if you don't immediately secure a new date.

Avoid Places That Remind You of Them

Don't go to areas that make you think about them. This should go without saying, but maybe you need to be reminded. These might be the bars you and she used to frequent, the park where you two first met, or the neighborhood diner she frequents. In these locations, you face the chance of running into them, which is the last thing you want if you want to get past them. That is, in a sense, the unconscious driving force behind visiting locations like this. You secretly wish you could run into them. Your efforts will be wasted. Of course, even if they aren't, just thinking about them in connection with these places will make you think of them. It would be wise for you to seek out alternative haunts for the time being. Another restaurant to visit and another area of the park to loiter around.

Put An End to Your Fantasies

It's natural to find yourself wondering, "If only I hadn't done that" or "If only I had told them how I felt, then." Life will always be filled with regrets. But that doesn't mean you should let them fill your thoughts all the time. It doesn't assist to consider who or what is at fault or all the possibilities. No amount of thinking will change the past because it is already fixed. But dwelling on it constantly will hinder your recovery, and instead of getting over it in a matter of weeks, you might wind yourself worrying about them for years. Some people even have DECADES-long thoughts for someone they've never had. Don't belong to that group.

Remain Composed and Take Care of Your Relationship with Yourself

The importance of stillness for healing cannot be overstated. If your mind is chaotic, there is only one direction you can go: down, down, down in an endless circle. My relationship was deteriorating, and I often felt uptight. My confidence and self-worth were at an all-time low. You can probably relate to the fact that heartbreak does little to feed the heart and soul. Some of it was being helped by my medicine, but it was starting to get pricey, and I don't want to get dependent on drugs. I attempted this free breathwork video because I had nothing to lose and everything to gain, and the results were amazing. But first, let me ask you why I'm informing you about this before we continue. I'm a big proponent of sharing because I want other people to feel just as powerful as I do. And if it helped me, it might also be helpful to you.

Make A List of The Traits You Want in A Partner

Try to find your core. Take a few deep breaths, grab some paper, and try to jot down your perfect partner's qualities. Be truthful. Take a moment to breathe if you find yourself writing things that are overly similar to what you believe you have observed in them. Consider if you are truly describing them or whether you are simply projecting your ideal onto them because you are so enamored with them. Most of the time, it's a little bit of both. The person you've wanted so badly only exists in your imagination, and they aren't quite the ideal match for your values as you would have first believed.

Spend Time with People Who Make You Happy

Try to find a big group of people that you can get lost in. People you can laugh with without worrying about anything. It would help even more if they don't know the person you're trying to get over. So, you won't be reminded of their absence. Laughter is the best medicine, and humor has always been a great way to ease tension in the air. But it's also important what kind of jokes are being told. In our society, it's sad to say, but the last thing you need is humor that hurts someone's pride. It might be funny when someone else is being laughed at, but it won't help when it's you.

Tell Yourself You're Important

As was already said, a low sense of self-worth can be a big reason why you might latch on to someone. The answer is, of course, to try to improve how you feel about yourself. It not only helps you get over the people you missed out on and lost, but it also makes it easier for you to find another chance in the future. People do like partners who are confident and sure of themselves, after all. You can talk to yourself in the mirror and tell yourself how great you are. You are important.

You can also write down all the nice things people have said about you and look at them whenever you are feeling down. You need to keep in mind that your whole life, including your love life, is still ahead of you. Because it's true.

Pay Attention to Your Body

Both mental and physical health are connected. If your mental health is bad, you might not want to take care of your physical health. If you don't take care of your body, it will hurt your mind.

And to get over someone, whether or not you date them, it's important to keep your health in good shape. Even if ignoring your body is tempting, it will only make it harder for you to get over them. So, go look up what healthy foods are available in your area. Spend some time every day working out, even if it's just jogging up and down the stairs or doing push-ups. But be careful not to do too much. It's easy to find too much comfort in food and gain weight or to find comfort in the wrong food and hurt your kidneys, your bank account, or both.

Give Yourself A Break

You might want to blame yourself for being such a "fool" for falling in love with someone who was obviously not right for you. Maybe they were too good for you, or maybe you could tell right away that they didn't like you. But in reality, it's fine.

You dreamed and hoped, and no one can blame you for that. So many people don't have the courage to do that, and they end up missing out on something better. You can think of it this way: you miss some of the shots you take, and you miss all of the shots you don't take. And it's human to make mistakes too. Anyone can make a mistake, but it only becomes a failure if you don't learn from it.

Give Time A Chance

In the end, you can't speed up the healing process. You can do everything you can to make it easier, but you can't control how long it will take you to heal. For example, some people are just built to be a bit more obsessive than others. Then, it's just easier for someone who's been hurt more than once to get over it than for someone who's just been hurt once or twice. It might take you a while to get better, and you might get frustrated if you feel like you're not making much progress, but at least you can take comfort in the fact that you'll get better faster the next time.

Conclusively, simply put, you are experiencing heartbreak. And it applies equally whether you were dating anybody or not. Although it can be difficult to let go of someone for whom you have strong feelings, there are several things you can do to speed up your recovery. The most crucial things are to keep yourself active and to take care of your health and mind. Fortunately, it's still simpler to move on from someone you've never dated than it is from someone you've dated.

Nothing was lost since you never had it in the first place. Though it may still exist, your emotional investment in them isn't as great as it could be. Finally, it's important to remember that even though it hurts right now, it will pass, and one day you'll just look back on this version of yourself and think, "Dang, what a lovestruck fool I was!"

CHAPTER FIVE

YOUR EX REACHED OUT?

THE MOST POSSIBLE REASONS WHY YOUR EX REACHED OUT AND DISAPPEARED

Did your ex contact you and have a conversation with you but then ignore you? I know, it's so perplexing, particularly when you're already attempting to advance. It might be irritating to try to figure out why an ex would bother to contact you before disappearing once more. What gives with that conflicting activity, then?

Let me explain the main causes for your ex's outreach and subsequent disappearance. After a breakup, it's common for an ex to get in touch with you and end the conversation abruptly.

Even if you both agreed to a "No Contact rule" during a breakup, this still occurs. Let's begin immediately.

They Miss You in Some Way

It hasn't ended yet. It's clear that your ex misses you when they utilize arbitrary justifications to get in touch with and message you.

Some indications that your ex misses you are as follows:

Your ex is curious about how your life is going.

Your ex requests a date with you

Your ex comes right out and says he misses you.

Your ex is irritated and envious that you're dating someone else. It's possible that your ex hasn't moved on from the split or still has feelings for you.

However, this does not necessarily imply that your ex wants to reconcile.

Your Ex Is Wounded Emotionally

Breakups are, to put it mildly, traumatic and distressing. Men are also not wired the same way as women are to deal with breakups. Your ex may be trying to contact you because they think of you as the "phantom ex" or the one who vanished. It's possible that your ex-girlfriend or boyfriend is still feeling hurt, sorry, disappointed, and confused. Your ex can still be stuck in this stage and be looking for excuses to meet up with you or try to get back together. Don't get too excited, especially if you haven't completely moved on from your ex.

Your Ex Is Lonely

When men are feeling low, they especially need an ego boost. He's prepared when they call or text you (and you respond), as he merely needed assurance that he still had it. He does not need to continue speaking with you because your response was adequate. On the other side, when a former flame makes an effort, women are flattered. We all likely have a small part of us that wishes for more communication, messages, or perhaps a fresh start. Are you still friends with your ex and wish to resume your previous relationship? You only have one option in this scenario: reignite their romantic interest in you.

There's A Need to Fulfill

No matter who ended the relationship, you can't get over the other person that quickly or misses them less. Just like you, your ex will get upset when random things remind them of the past. When your ex contacts you and you answer, they know you're still interested and can be reached. Reaching out to you is a way for them to get in touch with you.

Some of the possible reasons are:

They could be reaching out to make friends.

They could be trying to get help.

They might be killing time or getting rid of boredom.

They might be seeing if they like you enough to hook up with you for sex.

Your Ex-Lover Wants to Brag

Some men might brag about the women in their lives to boost their egos, become more popular, or seem more desirable. Others have a narcissistic personality and keep in touch with their ex-partners to get praise, sex, or to feel like they are important. Attention! He isn't interested in what you have to say because all he wants is a response from you. When he sends you a message, he wants your answer to make him look good. He would tell his friends about these conversations to prove that he was hot and desirable. Or maybe he just shows up out of the blue to show off. No matter what it is, be careful.

They Got A Few Drinks

When you drink, your inhibitions go down, and it can make you feel sad. When your ex-lover texts you after having a few drinks, it could mean:

They need approval, an ego boost, or love.

They still have unresolved feelings or need to put an end to things.

They want to make love.

They might miss you and be looking for you.

They don't know what they want and are bored.

When you're on the receiving end, you'll wonder if it's true. But, just like when drunk people text or call, nothing comes of it. It's done without much thought, and people always feel bad about it afterward. So don't worry about it.

He Feels Sentimental and Nostalgic

When a relationship ends, it can be hard to know how to feel. It's one of the most upsetting and stressful things that can happen, and grief can sometimes stop you from moving. Like women, men get sentimental and nostalgic too. Your ex might miss you because they remember the good times you had together. To deal with it, he'll send you a message or call you to see how you're doing or to tell you he's thinking about you. Your ex is giving in to the principle of nostalgia. It's a place where they might want to remember the best parts of their relationship.

But this can only last for a short time, no matter how strong it is. Soon, he'll be thinking or remembering something else. So, you have no reason to get attached when your ex calls you out of the blue.

Your Ex Is Overly Inquisitive

Your ex may be contacting you out of pure curiosity. They could have heard something intriguing about you, seen your social media posts, seen you eating dinner with someone, etc.

Your ex is interested in learning what is going on in your life.

The following examples of the reasons:

to understand how you're adjusting to the split

To learn more about the person you're going out with and how you feel about them

to be aware of your extracurricular activities

Don't get your hopes up because your ex is only getting in touch with you because he wants to know those things.

Your Ex Got Dumped or Broke Up Recently

If your ex contacts you by phone or text without warning, he might be hurt. He was likely dumped by someone, or he may have ended things with his present flame. He's getting back in touch with you so he can chat to you and, even for a split second, feel loved. He feels a glimmer of joy when he contacts you. It's because he thinks of you as someone he can rely on and because he's lonely. But this is only a transient solace, just like any other indicator. You won't hear from him once he is feeling better.

To Move on Without Regret

Your ex undoubtedly wants to know how you'll respond if he contacts you but doesn't respond after reading your response. Your ex is trying to get a reaction out of you in this situation, whether it's favorable or negative, so he can know how you feel and think about him. After you broke up, your ex is looking for some sort of post-breakup empowerment and validation. And after you say it, the final piece of the puzzle will be filled in by your words.

Recognize that it's intentional for your ex to contact you.

Give your ex what he wants, please.

Don't intentionally put your ex in a bad situation or make him feel bad, angry, or guilty. Free yourself from guilt and let your ex go.

Why does your ex keep getting in touch with you and then vanish? There are explanations for why your ex engages in ghosting so frequently. His current #1 priority is not you.

Your ex is preoccupied with family, job, or personal matters.

Your ex wants to maintain the current state of affairs.

Your ex doesn't know how you feel.

Your ex doesn't want to talk to you anymore.

Your ex is taking precautions to avoid getting close to you once more.

What should you do if your ex contacts you but then vanishes? It can be challenging to get over an ex, especially if you continue to hear from them. Try not to interpret your ex's frequent communications as meaning; if you do, you'll wind up feeling bewildered and perplexed. Keep in mind the main reason your relationship ended. Although you are not required to reply, doing so can still provide just as much information as doing so.

Be certain of what you hope to gain from the interaction before you answer.

You might think about doing the following:

Don't answer any calls or messages.

Answer in a relaxed, impartial manner.

Try to be as normal as you can

When you hear from your ex, resist the urge to celebrate.

Take a break if necessary.

Never overthink or dissect this situation.

Directly inquire as to why.

Whatever you do, don't anticipate anything to happen. Don't anticipate reuniting any time soon. Knowing what is best for you is most essential. Consider how you can mend your emotions. Make sure to maintain your limits whether you respond or not.

Keep in mind that letting go is usually a sign of strength.

CHAPTER SIX

WHAT IT MEANS WHEN A MAN AVOIDS EYE CONTACT WITH A WOMAN

Have you ever wondered why eye contact conveys attraction? Or why "love at first sight" instead of "love at first sight"? Beyond that, what if a man avoids eye contact with a woman? So, what does that mean? Let's dig in and find out together. The meaning and importance of eye contact

Like all nonverbal cues, eye contact is an essential part of communicating with others. This means that you are actively listening to what the other person is saying. On the other hand, one way people express indifference is by avoiding eye contact. When you're attracted to someone and you're making eye contact a lot, you're basically exposing yourself. It can actually be a great move. There are a few things science can tell us about eye contact. For example, it is much more difficult to know what someone means or thinks if they are blind.

Another fact about eye contact is that it helps our memory. When you can make eye contact, you are better able to remember what someone said and are ready to receive more and new information. Some people call eye contact actually oxytocin, the happiness chemical, or the “love hormone.” Oxytocin is involved in good emotional states and social and sexual bonding. The importance of eye contact isn't just limited to friendships and love, it's also helpful in the workplace. As? Let's see a real example. If you're in a job interview and you're not making eye contact with the person you're interviewing, they may think you're distracted and unenthusiastic about the opportunity. Making eye contact shows that you are an active listener, that you are confident, and most importantly, that you can trust them.

When you meet someone new, it's normal to make eye contact and smile. If you make eye contact instead and they don't return it, they may feel like they aren't interested in getting to know you or talking to you. In this case, you feel a sense of trust and sincerity. Still, it can be a way to assert dominance or intimidate someone, much like an athlete before a boxing match. Of course, if this is in a romantic context...

Red flag!

What is someone hiding if they don't make eye contact with you? As is often the case when examining body language, there are many reasons for avoiding eye contact. To the point: Here is a list of the most common meanings.

You may suffer from social anxiety or similar psychological problems. Some people with autism cannot make eye contact.

Maybe they don't have high self-esteem and are shy. Something makes them feel terrible and they're trying not to show it to you. They don't make eye contact because they are attracted to you...and you may be attracted to someone else and not make eye contact. Yes, see you soon!

They were exposed and unprepared for it. Unexpected changes startle or embarrass people so much that they stop making eye contact. They subconsciously feel better than you. This feeling of dominance can lead to loss of eye contact or no eye contact at all. More on this later. First, let's focus on the reasons why men can avoid eye contact with women and analyze them in detail.

HIDDEN REASONS WHY MEN DON'T MAKE EYE CONTACT WITH WOMEN

It's not well known, but actually, men are often shy. If they think you're beautiful and they're intimidated, they don't make eye contact for a long time or don't make eye contact at all. For this reason, it is important to know the clues that reveal the meaning behind this behavior. This way you reduce the chance of misinterpreting things. Let's explore why this is happening.

He's Crushing So Hard

It's often said that men who look up to you will be intimidated by you on the first date, and this may be true. Show and body language let it go. Some of these signs are:

Their pupils dilate when they are near you.

When they realize they are looking at you, they will look away.

You laugh, see if you laugh too, and share a joke.

In some cases, even more, blinking can be a sign that the other person is in love with you. If you catch emotions too, make more eye contact with them and see what happens!

You Don't Trigger His Inner Hero

Sometimes he needs that extra boost to make him notice you and want you. Especially when something goes wrong, like when he avoids eye contact with you. For men, it's all about unleashing your inner hero. I learned it from my heroic instinct. Created by relationship experts, this fascinating concept is about what drives men into relationships, and it's ingrained in their DNA. And that's what most women don't know. Once triggered, these drivers make men the heroes of their lives. They feel better, love more, and commit more when they find someone who knows how to make it happen. You may be wondering why it is called "heroic instinct". Do men need to feel like superheroes and commit to women? Not at all. Forget Marvel. You don't have to play a damsel in distress or buy a man a cloak. It's all about saying the right thing so he knows he only wants you.

He's Too Nervous Around You

Again, many men are shy when it comes to approaching women. After all, being rejected is not a comfortable feeling. Add a little anxiety to the mix and a nervous breakdown is waiting to happen. For example, let's say you're on a date and a guy wants you to notice him. Maybe he likes you and is nervous. Make it easier for him! Try not to be too direct with eye contact and focus more on what they are saying than reading their body language and facial expressions.

He Is Sad About Something

We all want to avoid being seen when we are sad. Sometimes we don't want to be vulnerable or we are afraid of what people will see when they see us. Even famous men can do this. When he's sad, no matter the situation or nature, you can avoid eye contact. Don’t let him talk and burst his bubble. You can even tell him that you don't want him to pretend that everything is fine when he isn't.

He May Be Submissive

Now, that's the important point. Maybe you just met them or you've known them for a while, but suddenly they don't look you in the eye anymore. Maybe... Surprise her by taking matters into your own hands: ask her and take the lead! Have fun.

He Is Not Passionate About You

If the guy you're dating suddenly starts avoiding eye contact with you, it could be because the spark isn't flying anymore. It's not about ticking every box on a man's list of what makes a "perfect girl"." Instead, men choose women they like. These women evoke a sense of excitement and a desire to chase through their own words. Their infatuation is triggered by primal impulses deep in the male brain. It may sound crazy, but there is a word combination that evokes red-hot passion.

He Is Upset or Angry

As we have already established, eye contact is a gateway for expressing both negative and positive emotions. When someone is angry, they may not make eye contact with them. You can talk to him about it or leave him alone. See what's good for you. If the guy doesn't know you, is angry with you, and is open about it, move away and find a safer place. Better find out.

He Has Something He Wants to Hide from You

If someone does something wrong or forgets something important, they may feel guilty about it. There is a possibility that This is because they don't want you to catch them and confront them about it, and they don't make eye contact.

He Has Autism or Mental Illness

Neurological disorders, such as autism, can interfere with eye contact with other people because it can be very uncomfortable. Too much stimulation can make you feel sick. Mental illness has the same cause. Depression and anxiety make it difficult to get in touch with people.

He Is Thinking Deeply

Eye contact takes up space in our brain. Avoiding eye contact is just a way for people to be more focused when they are concentrating on something difficult. We are all trying to make the most of our mental resources. This often happens when trying to remember something. This is the best way to save brain power and get things done. This is related to the unique concept of heroic instinct mentioned earlier. When a man feels respected, helpful, and needed, he's more likely to be with you and won't hesitate to communicate or make eye contact when he's thinking of you. The part is that triggering your hero's instincts is as easy as knowing the right things to say about a text.

He Is Deliberately Ignoring You

Not making eye contact is the best way to ignore someone or show indifference. please think about it. Eye contact conveys vulnerability and caution, so avoiding it means the exact opposite. However, if the person you care about suddenly avoids eye contact, talk about it and see what happened.

He Is Socially Anxious

Many of us suffer from anxiety. It makes sense that this is the number one reason to avoid eye contact with others. People with social anxiety disorder don't make eye contact as much as other people because it is often in their heads. Essentially, you can refer to the fear of being rejected. The judgment of others can weigh heavily on socially anxious people. When people with social anxiety are with friends and loved ones, everything is fine. If they dare to date or meet someone new now, it becomes more difficult. So if a man tells you that he suffers from social anxiety, give him space to be himself and talk about things. Guys don't make eye contact: What's next? Rejection is uncomfortable It's an emotion, and one way to avoid it is to stop making eye contact. It’s not good to feel like someone is judging us. It can always mean that the person is distracted or detached from the conversation or topic. So here are some things to consider if your man doesn't make much eye contact. It is important to be aware of these situations! Are you in a busy bar? Is your partner overly excited about where you are? Is this normal behavior? Knowing a little more about him, I can give you a better answer. Maybe he's shy or sad and avoids making eye contact with anyone. Try to take more cues from body language. If he's shy but likes you, he may not be making eye contact, but his body is in sync with you. There's more to dating than eye contact When approaching someone like Sherlock Holmes and trying to figure out why he avoids eye contact, consider multiple clues. For simplicity, I created another list of characters.

This time, you'll know if he likes or dislikes you without making eye contact.

Most of the time his feet are pointing towards you.

He tries to be around you when you are in a group.

When he sees you, he will adjust his clothes or check his hair.

He mimics your movements and body language.

When he sees you, his demeanor changes.

He gets a little uneasy when he sees you talking to other men. He can be charming, intimidating, or submissive, but you'll know it when you notice him avoiding eye contact and body language letting him off. Now you can understand all of Sherlock Holmes's behavior. To be honest, I can see his body language for more than one reason. Attraction and submission can go hand in hand.

By now you should know why he avoids eye contact with you. The key now is to get through to your man in a way that empowers both him and you. We mentioned the concept of heroic instinct earlier - by working directly with his primal instinct, you can not only solve this problem but develop your relationship more than ever before.

CHAPTER SEVEN

REASONS WHY DATING IS SO IMPORTANT

In my mid-twenties, I got to the point where I was burned out by boring, unsatisfying dates. I vowed never to date again and just focused on my work. It's a promise, I'm glad I broke it. The list below includes ways to make the most out of dating and make it a rewarding experience, even though it rarely leads to long-term relationships.

Dating Lets You Discover Who You Are

Dating is very important because it allows you to discover who you are. Even if it's not satisfying, dating shows you a lot more about yourself, what you want, how much discipline you have, and how wrong you are. It reveals what you are willing to do and how committed you are to stay true to yourself. Dating is in many ways a blank canvas. Today, most people deal with it by downloading apps, logging into websites, and browsing who is available. However, you are under no obligation to do so. You can also invite your colleagues and see if sparks fly between you and your friends.

Dating Is What You Make of It

Like so much in life, dating is what you make of it. When faced with an unsatisfying experience or lack of chemistry, it can be tempting to give up, as I have been for a while. Eventually, though, I became a little more selective about what I was looking for, avoiding dates, and getting better at meeting women I wasn't interested in. Dating people, I didn't want to date. Remember, you are under no obligation to do so. It's always better to break up or turn down a date than to seduce someone. Dating inevitably leads to disappointments, but it can also provide all sorts of valuable and sometimes enjoyable experiences that can help you find a serious partner.

Dating Can Help You Find What You're Looking For

Dating is also a way to find what you're looking for. You may start off in a haze, but dating a few people will give you a clearer picture of what attracts you and what doesn't. Nevertheless, the dating process can be very confusing and stressful, especially if you can't find what you're looking for. Want advice tailored to your situation? While this chapter looks at the top reasons why dating is so important, it may be helpful to talk to a relationship coach about your situation. You can get advice specific to...

Dating Teaches Us the Value of Quality Over Quantity

The main reason I got bored with dating in my twenties was because I approached it like an all-you-can-eat buffet. I looked at some pictures and ignored everything the girl wrote before sending her a message or deleting them just because of her appearance. The result was extreme boredom and frustration. rice field. Even when someone was happy with their photos (or looked better), there was almost always a big downside. She would be very beautiful, but she would stand out quickly because she was psychotic and psychotic. It popped out of my skin. So, I switched to focusing on individuality. Then I ended up having a fascinating discussion of history and philosophy with someone I wouldn't kiss for millions of years. This means that it will teach you

Dating Provides You a Way to Work on Communication

Going on dates is one way to become a better communicator. In my case, I learned to express myself more clearly and be a better listener. I was used to growing up in a good school. Dating has taught me to slow down a little, listen, and be a little more patient. I also learned a lot about being more patient with things I disagree with, things I find boring or unacceptable, and offensive or silly. I'm not pretending to agree. It means that you don't immediately react positively or negatively to what someone says. This is a very good skill to have in many areas of life, especially in business and love.

It Offers Opportunities to Be More Romantic

A date should be romantic. For those of us who tend to be more platonic or clinical, it can be a great time to warm up our more romantic side. It's your effort that counts, even if you have to google it. A date is your chance to become a more romantic person by paying attention to the atmosphere you create with your setup, words, actions, and choices. It helps you know what to do and what not to do. Being a more romantic person is something your future husband or wife will appreciate you for. will be highly evaluated.

Dating Brings Out the Best and Worst in You

I'm not always the best dater and have had some embarrassing weaknesses. For one thing, I don't react well to rejection. I remember being angry when I threw away a gift from one date. Later, he said that he liked me like a friend, but I didn't feel compatible. This coffee mug bore the brunt of my immature rage. My best? Well, I don't want to blow my own horn (that's what people often say before I blow my own horn), but I think dating has made me a better listener and more patient. I also feel more confident in showing my feelings, speaking the truth about what I feel and believe, and being more determined.

Dating Gets You Offline for A While

I don't know about you, but spending too much time online is one of my biggest sins. Dating can help in that it will at least take you offline for a while. limit:

During the pandemic, many started going out on virtual dates. A friend of mine met her boyfriend that way. Do everything for her! But I think there's something about face-to-face dating that's hard to find with virtual or remote dating. Now that many countries have reopened, dating offers the opportunity to meet in person again. Having a cup of coffee or playing mini golf You can do classic things like hanging out, eating out, and watching a movie. We recommend keeping it simple. Many also point out that activities such as watching a movie are fairly passive and don't give you much opportunity to get to know this new person or create sparks.

Dating Teaches You How to Respect Yourself

Through repeated unsatisfying dates, I learned how to be more selective and respect myself. I became more patient and a better listener, but I also learned to respect my boundaries. In some cases, I cut off contact with people who asked me out on dates. Also, it was just to be honest that I'm not crazy about girls. Dating teaches us to be more honest and respectful of ourselves and our boundaries. Especially when you push them and try to burn yourself. If you're struggling with frustration in a relationship, have you ever considered getting to the root of the problem? Most of our shortcomings in love stem from our complicated inner relationships with ourselves.

If you want to improve your relationships with others and resolve dating confusion and frustrations, start with yourself first.

Dating Can Be Fun Sometimes

I've talked quite a bit about some of my complaints about dating and boredom in this article. Whether it's board games or kissing outdoors, dating can be a fun experience. Overcoming fear and becoming more confident is one of the best benefits of dating. But another great thing is meeting people you wouldn't otherwise know and having conversations, interactions, and experiences you might otherwise miss.

Dating eases conflict

Another often overlooked reason, why dating is important, is that it makes conflict feel more comfortable. What I'm trying to say is that I've had a lot of dates where things didn't go so well and I didn't want to see them again. I've gotten much better at going to. Admittedly, I haven't always responded well to rejection, and I still don't. However, I am no longer shy about letting someone down or feeling like I have to show interest. Contradiction is OK. Dating shows that you can respect someone even if you think they're wrong and you're not romantically interested. And that is a valuable lesson to learn.

Dating Makes You More Sociable

Dating takes you out into the big wide world and conversations with other people. It’s a very good thing in itself. Especially since there is so much temptation to wrap yourself up in internet echo chambers and social media and avoid meeting new people. Going out there and taking risks is a daring act, especially these days. You get out there, test the water and you are a real human being. It deserves recognition! And it's worth it. To be up to date or not to be up to date, that is the question. Dating can be frustrating, but it can also be rewarding. When deciding how to approach dating, remember that how you perceive it is up to you. It is imperative to be selective, but try to be open about what you are going through. Dating is a way to meet many new and interesting people, as well as those with whom you want to build long-term relationships. Like Dr. Greg Smalley writes.

www.ingramcontent.com/pod-product-compliance
Lightning Source LLC
LaVergne TN
LVHW012116170826
845678LV00014BA/2963

* 9 7 9 8 8 4 7 5 1 2 9 0 9 *